Birth and Early Years of Gandhiji's Life

Mahatma Gandhi is one of the most revered names in Indian history. He was the political and ideological leader of India, also honoured as Father of our nation, he became an international symbol of the free India. He played a very important role in the Indian freedom movement. He is lovingly called as Bapu. His teachings of 'Ahinsa' and 'Satya' (non-violence and truth) changed the complete outlook of the Indian freedom fighters.

Mohan Das Karamchand Gandhi, also known as Mahatma Gandhi, was born on 2nd October 1869 in a Hindu family of Porbandar, Gujarat. His parents were Karamchand Gandhi and Putlibai.

His father, Karamchand Gandhi was a Diwan (Chief Minister) of Porbandar and an honourable and upright man. Gandhiji's mother was a religious and pious woman. Gandhiji gained high moral and social values from his parents. Since childhood, Gandhiji believed strongly in non-violence, truth, purity and very simple lifestyle.

At the age of 13, Gandhiji got married to a girl of the same age named, Kasturba Gandhi. They had four sons. Gandhiji started his education in Porbandar. He further studied in Rajkot and did his matriculation. Then, he joined the University of Bombay in 1887. His family wanted him to become a barrister.

In 1888, he went to London for further studies and completed his law in 1891. He returned to India. For the next two years, he practised law in India.

Gandhiji in South Africa

At the age of 23, Gandhiji left his family once again and came to South Africa as a legal advisor of an Indian businessman. In South Africa, Gandhiji found that there was a strong demarcation between the Black and White communities. The Black community faced a lot of discrimination and were very badly treated. Gandhiji felt very bad about this.

Just after a week of his stay, Gandhiji experienced the humiliation because of discrimination. One day, he had to travel in a train. He had a first-class ticket with him. At the Pietermartizburg station when he entered the first-class compartment and was asked to shift to the third-class compartment. The ticket checker told him that the first-class was reserved for Whites.

On raising objection on this discrimination, Gandhiji was thrown out of the train.

During this journey, he late came to know that discrimination is the common practise there. The Black community and the Indians were called 'coolies'.

After this incident, Gandhiji decided to fight against this injustice. He wrote letters to the higher officials and began a protest against the discrimination in South Africa.

For the next three years, Gandhiji continuously fought for the justice. Soon, he became a well-known activist and a leader of the Indian community.

On 22nd May 1894, Gandhiji established an organisation—Natal Indian Congress (NIC) in South Africa. This organisation looked after the rights of Indians living there. While working for NIC, Gandhiji also faced a lot of opposition from the other communities. He was also attacked several times.

Gandhiji spent twenty years in South Africa. Thereafter, in the year 1915, he returned to India.

Gandhiji in India

Gandhiji's struggles and successes in South Africa were well known in India also. He became a 'National Hero' in the eyes of Indians. Gandhiji wanted to create the same wave of reformation in India. He travelled to all the parts of India to know the real conditions of Indians.

While his travels, Gandhiji used to wear a dhoti and wooden slippers. He renounced all the pleasures and adopted a very simple lifestyle.

He established the 'Sabarmati Ashram' in Ahmedabad, Gujarat. He lived in the ashram with his family and some of his supporters. Everyone loved and supported Gandhiji.

People started believing in his teachings of non-violence and truth. He got the title of 'Mahatma', which meant 'a great soul'.

The Indian Freedom Movement

India was under British rule at that time. A large number of freedom fighters were fighting for the freedom of India. Gandhiji also wanted the freedom of India but he followed a different path. He began a non-violent movement called 'Satyagraha' against the British.

Satyagraha means opposition, but not in an aggressive form. Gandhiji taught people to ask for justice in a silent way. The movement created a strong wave and became a great success.

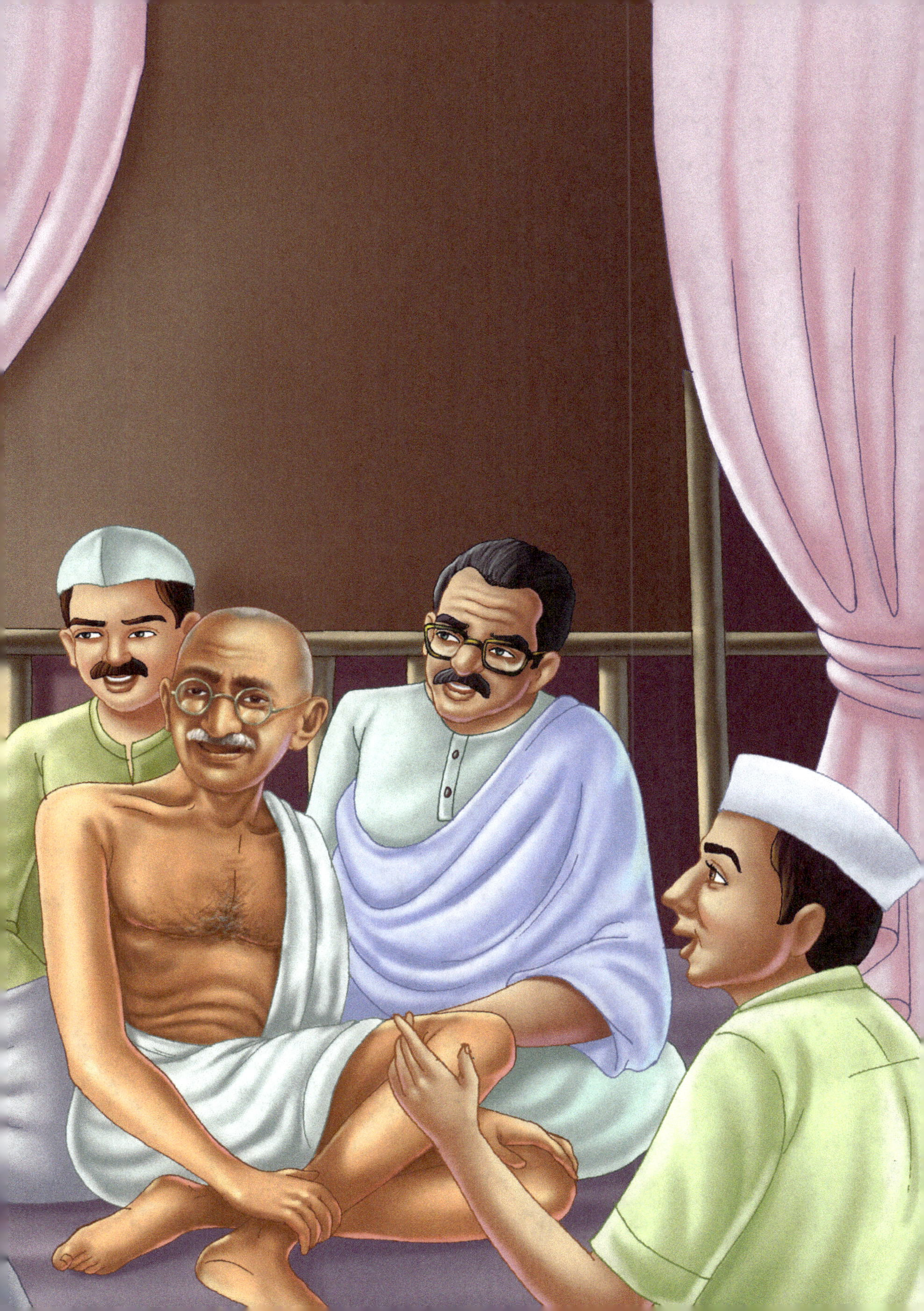

In 1919-20, Gandhiji started another movement called 'Non-cooperative movement'. During his struggle for freedom, Gandhiji was sent to jail many times by the British Govt, but he continued his mission. He asked indians to stop using foreign clothes and other things. He insisted to spin natural cloth on Charkha (spinning wheel). The image of the Charkha later became a symbol of the Indian independence.

On 12th March 1930, Gandhi ji began 'Dandi March' or the 'Salt March' against the salt tax. Gandhi ji with his supporters stand walking 200 miles from Sabarmati Ashram towards the sea.

On April 5, the group reached Dandi, a place along the Coast. Gandhiji demonstrated the method to make salt from the seawater. Soon, the movement spread in the entire nation. Gandhiji was imprisoned once again but, the protest continued nationwide. It was stopped only after the 'Delhi Pact' between the British Government and Gandhiji. The Pact granted the limited salt production and all the protestors were released.

In 1942, Gandhiji issued the last call for independence from British rule. He initiated another movement called 'August Kranti.' Soon after, he began 'Quit India' movement that asked the Britishers to leave India.

After the long struggle and sacrifices, India became independent on 15th August 1947. At the time of freedom, India faced the partition in two parts. After the freedom, Gandhiji tried to maintain peace and unity among the people of different communities.

There was a lot of disturbance in all the parts of country. The communal violence was spreading fast. To stop this violence, Gandhiji began a 'fast unto death' on 13th January 1948 which proved to be a success. On 18th January 1948, he ended his fast only when he got the assurance that the communal violence would be stopped.

Assassination of Gandhiji

Some Indians believed that Gandhiji was responsible for the partition of India. Gandhiji faced a lot of opposition. On the unfortunate day of 30th January 1948, Gandhiji was going to address a prayer meeting. He was walking along with his two assistants—Abha and Manu. Just when he was stepping towards the stage to address the public, a man named Nathuram Godse fired at Gandhiji. Gandhiji fell on the ground, saying, "Hey Ram, Hey Ram!" These were the last words of Mahatma Gandhi.

The great soul, the light of the nation, was gone. The whole country was mourning bitterly on their dear Bapu's departure from the world. The other countries were also shocked at his death.

Soon after the assassination of Mahatma Gandhi, Pt. Jawahar Lal Nehru addressed the nation on radio:
"Friends & Comarades, The light has gone out of our lives and there is darkness everywhere. I do not know what to tell you and how to say it. Our beloved leader, Bapu as we called him, the Father of the Nation, is no more.
Perhaps I am wrong to say that. Nevertheless, we will never see him again as we have seen him for these many years. We will not run to him for advice and seek solace from him, and that is a terrible blow, not only to me, but also to millions and millions in this country.
And it is a little difficult to soften the blow by any other advice that I or anyone else can give you.."

India Remembers Mahatma Gandhi

Mahatma Gandhi's Samadhi is at Raj Ghat in Delhi. Thousands of people from all over the country come to Raj Ghat to pay homage to the great man.

2nd October, Gandhiji's birthday is celebrated as 'Gandhi Jayanti'. It is one of the three National festivals of India. People of India still remember their dear 'Bapu' with great love and reverence.

Every year, 30th January—the day of Gandhiji's assassination, is observed as the Martyr's Day to commemorate the struggle of all those who sacrificed their life for the country. Mahatma Gandhi's picture is also printed on the Indian currency notes.

Mahatma Gandhi was a great writer also. He wrote and edited many newspaper articles during his lifetime. He also wrote several books including his autobiography—My Experiments with Truth.

In the year 1930, Time magazine named Mahatma Gandhi as 'The Man of the Year'. There are many books written about him and his teachings. The life of Mahatma Gandhi has been widely portrayed in the Indian literature, theatre and movies.

Mahatma Gandhi dedicated his entire life for the welfare of Indians. He has been the greatest source of inspiration for all the Indians. His teachings of non-violence, peace and truth are still practised and followed by many, not only in India but also in other countries.

The only way to pay tribute to the great man—The Father of Our Nation—is to follow his teachings in our lives. We should learn from the great life of Mahatma Gandhi.

Birth and Early Years of Gurudev's Life

Rabindra Nath Tagore is one of the most popular and respected names in the field of Indian literature and music. Famous as Sobriquet Gurudev, he was a renowned poet, musician, writer, educationist, painter and social reformer.

Rabindra Nath Tagore was born in Kolkata (known as Calcutta earlier) in an affluent Bengali Brahmin family on 7th May 1861. He was the youngest of the thirteen children of his parents—Debendra Nath Tagore and Sharda Devi.

Since childhood, Rabindra Nath Tagore was inclined towards literature and music. He loved reading and spending time in library. At a very young age, he started reading the works of Kalidas and other famous Indian poets.

At the age of eight, Rabindra Nath Tagore wrote his first poetry. His parents were very proud to see his extraordinary skills and talent.

At the age of twelve, Rabindra Nath Tagore got an opportunity to visit many places of India with his father. He visited his father's Shantiniketan estate in Bholapur. And after that, he visited Punjab, Himachal Pradesh and Himalayas. This tour of India had a great impact on his young mind. He was fascinated to see the natural beauty and the rich culture of India.

Rabindra Nath Tagore aspired to read more and more about Indian culture, nature and many more topics related to India. He was not much interested in his school studies. But his father wanted him to go out for higher studies to become a barrister.

Rabindra Nath Tagore's father bought a big house in Dalhousie—a place very close to the nature. Rabindra Nath Tagore was very happy to see the natural beauty of the place. Once, he expressed his love for nature and poetry to his father.

He said, "Baba, I just love to be in the lap of nature. I want to write about each and every beautiful thing of the nature."

"Yes. Dear Son, nature is full of the beauty and wonders. But I want you to concentrate more on your studies and become a barrister rather than wasting time in watching the sights and writing poems," replied Debendra Nath.

Debendra Nath was extremely worried to see Rabindra Nath's inclination towards the literature. He started planning to send him abroad for higher studies.

Rabindra Nath Tagore in Britain

In the year 1878, Rabindra Nath Tagore's father sent him to Britain for higher studies. He was only seventeen years old at that time. His elder brother Satyendra Nath was also with him.

Rabindra Nath got admission in a good school in London. After the school, he was admitted in the University of London. He was multitalented. He loved the new environment and learnt many new things in London. He was fond of the music.

He liked the western music a lot and soon learnt it nicely. Within a few months, he started composing wonderful songs and music.

Rabindra Nath was not serious for the higher studies. He could not complete his education and returned to India without completing degree.

Rabindra Nath's Return to India

In 1880, Debendra Nath called Rabindra Nath to come back to India. Rabindra Nath, on returning, pursued his interest in literature. He wrote a set of poetries and got it published for the first time. His work was hugely recognised and appreciated in Kolkata.

The admiration boosted Rabindra Nath's confidence to a great extent. He started devoting more and more time in reading and writing.

In 1884, Rabindra Nath experienced immense grief when his sister-in-law, Kadambari Devi, suddenly died. Rabindra Nath was very close to his sister-in-law. She was the one who took utmost care of him like her own child, after his mother's death.

This incident shattered Rabindra Nath. His sister-in-law was like a strong pillar in his life. She was also a friend and a mentor to him. She always encouraged him to pursue his love for literature and music.

Rabindra Nath decided to create something great and dedicate it to Kadambari Devi. He wrote a wonderful collection of verses named 'Bhanusimher Padavali', which proved to be a literary wonder at that time. He dedicated this great work to Kadambari Devi.

'Shaishav Sangeet' was his other creation that was dedicated to Kadambari Devi.

Great Works of Rabindra Nath Tagore

In the year 1883, Rabindra Nath got married to Bhavtarini Devi. After the marriage, she was given another name, Mrinalini Devi. Marriage brought a beautiful phase in Rabindra Nath's life. He lived very happily with his wife.

Rabindra Nath's passion for writing was continued to prosper even after his marriage. He gave great creative works one after the other. He also wrote some great plays.

All of his creations became very famous and were very much admired in the world of Indian Literature.

The life of villagers, and the lifestyle of Bengalees inspired Rabindra Nath to write short stories. His stories were also highly admired.

In the year 1891, Rabindra Nath had to shoulder his father's responsibilities of being a Zamindar. He took the charge of their family estates in Shelaidaha. He performed his duties of Zamindari with full dedication. And soon, he became the most lovable and respectfull name among the people. By this time, he was blessed with five children—two sons and three daughters.

In the year 1901, Rabindra Nath left Shelaidaha and moved to Bholapur Shantiniketan. There, he opened a school—Shantiniketan Brahmacharya Ashram. One of the first five students of this school was Bhavani Chandra Chaterjee. He was a great disciple of Rabindra Nath and he fondly called him, 'Gurudev.'

Soon, Rabindra Nath became popular by a sobriquet Gurudev. Shantiniketan was running successfully. But in 1902, his life was again clouded with the sorrows. His dear wife Mrinalini Devi died after a long illness. Rabindra Nath was completely broken. But soon, he got over from his grief and focused once again on his work.

At that time, India was under British Rule. Rabindra Nath Tagore was also concerned about India's freedom. He contributed in the freedom fight by writing inspirational poetries about India and the freedom fighters. 'Navedya' and 'Kheya' were his most popular patriotic writing. His speech, 'Swadesi Samaj' is still remembered. He also wrote many articles on freedom fights and the nation, which ignited the emotions of patriotism in his readers. Rabindra Nath once visited London with his son. During his journey, a great idea struck his mind. He thought, "How nice it would be to spread India's glory and rich culture in other countries also!"

This thought of Gurudev inspired him to create his literary masterpiece, 'Gitanjali'. In this masterpiece, he translated hundreds of his patriotic poetries in English. The great artist Rothenstein and the famous poet W. B. Yeats were impressed to see the Gurudev's poetry. W. B. Yeats wrote a beautiful introduction for Gitanjali.

On getting published in 1912, 'Gitanjali' created a wave of excitement in England. The People of England became great fans of Gurudev and his poetry.

Rabindra Nath Tagore was the first Indian to receive the Noble Prize, in the year 1913, for his outstanding contribution in literature.

After the achievement of Noble Prize, Gurudev was also honoured by the prestigious title of 'Sir' by the British Government. This is the first time any Indian was offered a knighthood.

Apart from his contribution in the literature, he also gifted a unique form of the music called Rabindra Sangeet to the Indian society.

There was no field of art that remained untouched by multitalented Gurudev. He also created marvellous paintings and sketches. Many exhibitions were held to display his great work.

Rabindra Nath was also a social worker. He tried to eradicate many ill social practises and issues. He also worked and spread awareness to end the culture of 'Untouchability'.

During his lifetime, Gurudev met many famous personalities like Einstein, Mussolini and H. G. Wells.

Gurudev wrote a large number of poems, stories, articles, speeches and songs in his lifetime.
During the last years of his life, he also wrote his autobiography.
The Indian national anthem, 'Jana gana mana', was also written by Rabindra Nath Tagore.

The Last Phase of Gurudev's Life

The pace of Gurudev's work did not slow down irrespective of his old age. He continued writing, reading, delivering lectures, social services and visiting foreign countries. His excessive involvement in work affected his body badly. His health started deteriorating day by day.

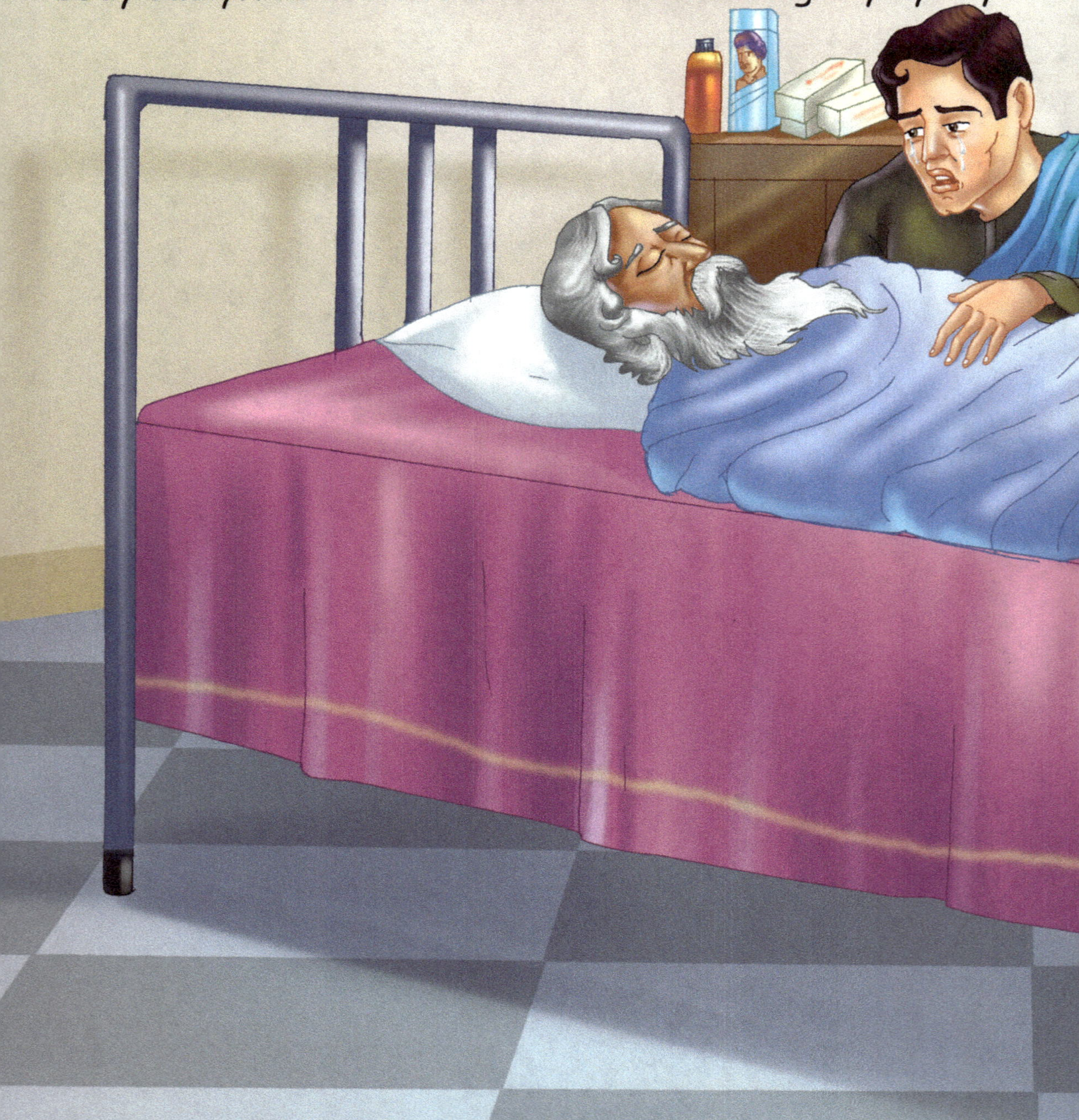

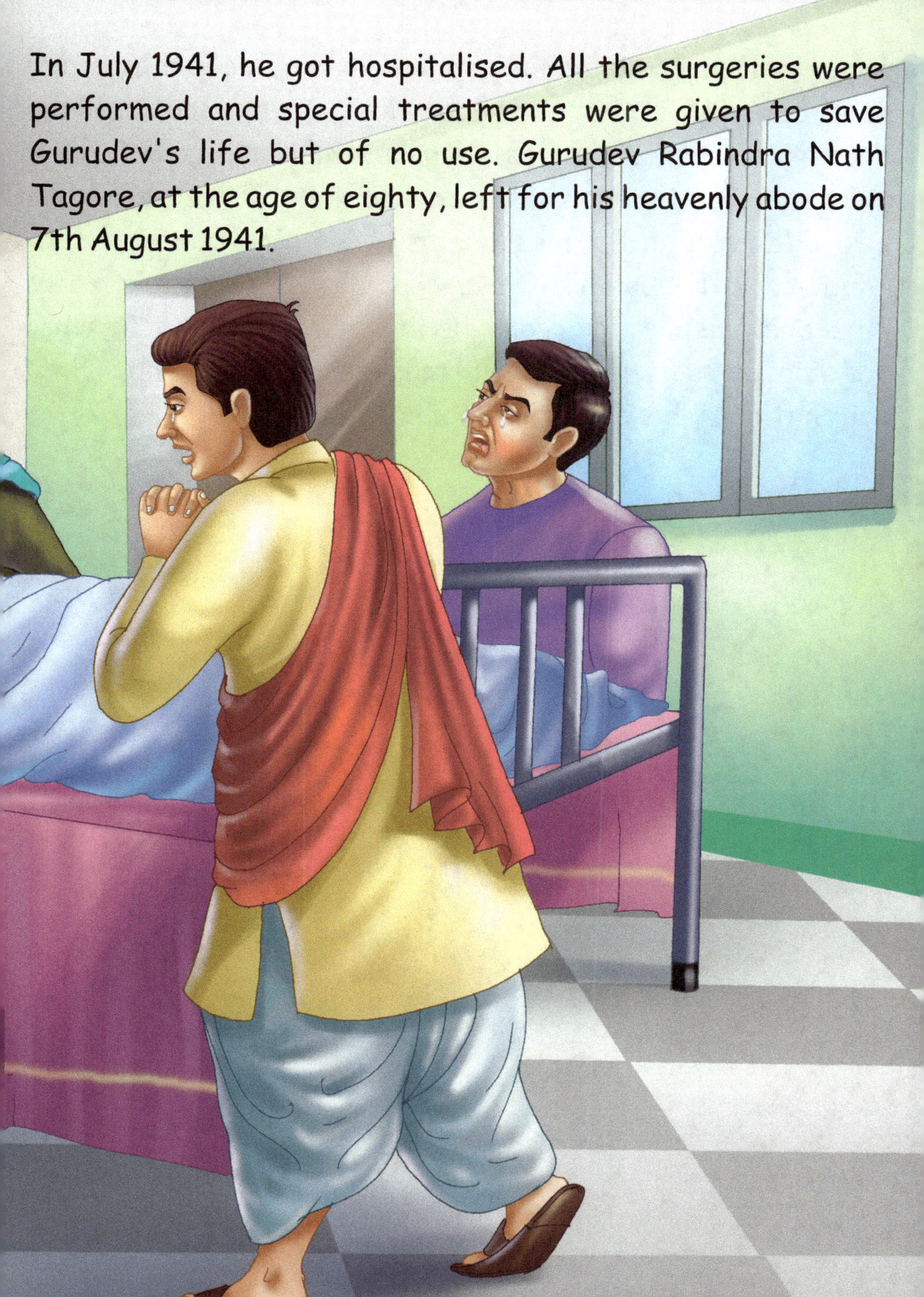

In July 1941, he got hospitalised. All the surgeries were performed and special treatments were given to save Gurudev's life but of no use. Gurudev Rabindra Nath Tagore, at the age of eighty, left for his heavenly abode on 7th August 1941.

His death was a big shock for millions of people in India and abroad. It was a very big loss for our nation. His poetries, dramas, stories, songs and music are still fondly remembered through out the country and also in abroad. Gurudev spread the message of love, unity, brotherhood and peace through his literary creations. We should learn and draw inspiration from the life of this great man, who dedicated his entire life in transforming and improving our nation by his incredible work.